Penguin Readers

HOW TO TURN DOWN A BILLION DOLLARS

THE SNAPCHAT STORY

BILLY GALLAGHER

LEVEL

2

D1420128

ADAPTED BY CATRIN MORRIS
SERIES EDITOR: SORREL PITTS

PENGUIN BOOKS

UK | USA | Canada | Ireland | Australia
India | New Zealand | South Africa

Penguin Books is part of the Penguin Random House group of companies
whose addresses can be found at global.penguinrandomhouse.com.
www.penguin.co.uk www.puffin.co.uk www.ladybird.co.uk

How to Turn Down a Billion Dollars: The Snapchat Story first published by Virgin Books,
an imprint of Ebury Publishing, 2018
This Penguin Readers edition published by Penguin Books Ltd, 2019

001

Original text written by Billy Gallagher
Text for Penguin Readers edition adapted by Catrin Morris
Text copyright © Billy Gallagher 2018, 2019
Cover design by Two Associates
Cover design copyright © Virgin Books, 2018

The moral right of the original author has been asserted

Photo credits
Pages 4 and 7 (Evan Spiegel) © J. Emilio Flores/*The New York Times*/Redux; pages 4 and 10 (Bobby Murphy)
© J. Emilio Flores/*The New York Times*/Redux; pages 4 and 19 (Mark Zuckerberg) © catwalker/Shutterstock.com;
pages 4 and 22 (Michael Lynton) © s_bukley/Shutterstock.com; pages 5 and 8 (Red Bull advert) ©
Clari Massimiliano/Shutterstock.com; pages 5 and 12 (apps on a phone) © Charnsitr/Shutterstock.com; pages 5
and 10 (computer code) Vintage Tone/Shutterstock.com; pages 5 and 14 (Ghostface Chillah logo) © Snap Inc;
pages 5 and 9 (Stanford University campus) © turtix/Shutterstock.com; page 18 (Snapchat's interface)
© Billy Gallagher/TechCrunch; page 19 (Steve Jobs) © Castleski/Shutterstock.com; (Bill Gates)
© JStone/Shutterstock.com; page 23 (Snapchat office) © 2013. Los Angeles Times. Used with permission.; page 24
(Facebook's Poke app) © Josh Constine/TechCrunch; page 29 (Snapchat Stories) © PixieMe/Shutterstock.com;
page 32 (QR code) © Zapp2Photo/Shutterstock.com; page 33 (Slingshot app) © Josh Constine/TechCrunch;
page 34 (Making videos at a live event) © Gansstock/Shutterstock.com; page 35 (Snapchat's geofilters)
© Josh Constine/TechCrunch; page 36 (The love story geofilter) © Snap Inc.; page 40 (DJ Khaled)
© Jamie Lamor Thompson/Shutterstock.com; (Shonduras) © Kathy Hutchins/Shutterstock.com; page 44
(Snapchat's first birthday) © Snap Inc.; page 45 (Snapchat lenses) © dennizn/Shutterstock.com; page 50
(Evan and his wife) © AP Photo/Andrew Harnick; page 52 (Snapchat Spectacles) © NYCStock/Shutterstock.com;
(Snapchat's pop-up shop) © Fitz Tepper/TechCrunch.

Printed and bound in Great Britain by Clays Ltd, Elcograf S.p.A.

A CIP catalogue record for this book is available from the British Library

ISBN: 978-0-241-39772-5

All correspondence to
Penguin Books
Penguin Random House Children's Books
80 Strand, London WC2R 0RL

Contents

People in the book

Evan Spiegel

Bobby Murphy

Mark Zuckerberg

Michael Lynton

New words

advertise

app

code

logo

university

website

Note about the book

This is the story of an **app*** called Snapchat that people can use to send **disappearing** photos to other people. "Snap" means taking photos, and "chat" means talking to friends. It is also the story of three friends: Evan Spiegel, Reggie Brown, and Bobby Murphy. Evan wanted to **design** a **website**. Reggie had an **idea** for an app. Bobby was a good **coder**. Together, they made Snapchat, and they made a lot of money. But they are not all **still** friends today.

Before-reading questions

1 What do you know about Snapchat? How is it different from other apps?

2 Look at the "People in the book" on page 4. Describe Evan or Bobby.

3 What do you think happens to Evan and Bobby in the book?

4 What do you know about Mark Zuckerberg?

5 What does Mark Zuckerberg do in the book, do you think?

*Definitions of words in **bold** can be found in the glossary on pages 61–63.

CHAPTER ONE
The "million-dollar idea"

Evan Spiegel **was born** on June 4th 1990, in Los Angeles, California.

Evan's parents were **lawyers**. His family lived in Pacific Palisades, a rich part of California. In the summer holidays, they helped to build houses for poor people in Mexico.

Evan Spiegel

At school, Evan loved computers, and he built his first computer at the age of eleven. He also loved writing, and he wrote for the school **newspaper**. **Companies advertised** in the newspaper because Evan talked nicely to them. They liked him.

In 2007, Evan was at **high school**. His parents were not together. Evan lived with his father in a very big and expensive house, and he had lots of parties there. Evan asked the drinks company Red Bull for a job. They did not pay him, but they did pay for his parties!

Red Bull advertised their drinks at Evan's parties.

In 2008, Evan started studying at Stanford **University**. He learned to **design** things for computers, and he lived in a room at the university. A student lived in the room opposite him. The student's name was Reggie Brown.

8

Stanford University

Reggie Brown was born on January 17th 1990, in South Carolina, in the south of the United States of America. He studied English at Stanford University.

Reggie liked parties, too, and he and Evan were good friends. They **joined** an important **club** together. The name of the club was Kappa Sigma. Bobby Murphy also joined the club.

Bobby Murphy was born in California, on July 19th 1988. His mother came from the Philippines.

Bobby studied mathematics and computers at Stanford University. He was very different from Evan Spiegel and Reggie Brown. He was older and quieter, and he did not go to many parties.

Bobby Murphy

Bobby could write computer **code**, and he made a **website** with Evan.

Computer code

This website could help high school students learn about universities. Evan asked students from the Kappa Sigma club for help with their website. People helped Evan because they liked him. But they did not like the website, because there was nothing really new about it.

In 2011, Evan went to South Africa, and Reggie went to study in Oxford. They came back to Stanford University, but things did not go well for them. They had to leave the Kappa Sigma club because of their loud parties. Then Evan's girlfriend left him, and Reggie did not do well at university.

But, one day, Reggie had an **idea** for a **social-media site**. He thought, "I'd like to send **disappearing** photos!"

He ran to Evan's room because he wanted to tell Evan about his idea. Evan listened and said, "That's a **million**-dollar idea!"

CHAPTER TWO

Picaboo

Evan liked Reggie's idea because it was different from other social-media sites. Other sites keep everything. Photos and messages stay on the internet.

At first, Evan and Reggie could not find any help. It was a **funny** idea, but nothing more. Then Evan asked Bobby Murphy to write the code for them. He said yes, and Evan, Reggie, and Bobby started working together.

Apps on a phone

First, they built a website. But, because the website was not very good, they built a phone **app**.

Bobby worked on the code. Evan designed the app. He wanted to know, "How do **users** use the app?" And Reggie thought of its name—Picaboo. The name came from a game called peekaboo.

They asked their friends to try using Picaboo. But, at that time, only people with **iPhones** could use it. It was a nice app, and people liked it, but nothing more.

The three friends wanted to make the app easier to use. They stayed at Evan's family home in the summer holidays, and they worked hard there.

Evan had lots of ideas about Picaboo. He wanted the camera to open with the app and be ready to take photos.

But he did not want the app to keep the photos. You could send photos, and your friends could look at them. But then the photos disappeared.

Evan also wanted a funny **logo**. Reggie and Evan designed the logo. It was yellow and white. The name of the logo was Ghostface Chillah.

A version of the Ghostface Chillah logo

Evan and Bobby worked very hard, but Reggie did not work as hard as his friends. Evan got angry with Reggie about this, and Reggie was not happy.

The Picaboo app was ready in July 2011. They

advertised it as "a game for sending disappearing pictures with your friends."

At this time, Evan and Bobby were in Bobby's house in California, and Reggie was at home in South Carolina. Reggie wrote the company's name, Picaboo, on an important **document**. And he wrote their three names on the document, too: Bobby Murphy, Reggie Brown, Evan Spiegel.

Reggie told Evan and Bobby about this on the phone. Evan was angry. He wanted only Bobby Murphy's name on the document because Bobby wrote the code for the app. Reggie did not do very much work on the app. And Evan did not want his name after Reggie Brown's name.

Evan and Bobby changed Picaboo's **passwords**. Now Reggie could not open the app. He was out of Picaboo.

CHAPTER THREE

Snapchat

In September 2011, Picaboo only had about one hundred users, but they used it a lot. Then Evan and Bobby had to change its name because there was a photo-book company called Picaboo. They chose a new name: Snapchat. "Snap" means photo, and "chat" means talking to friends. The Snapchat app was born on September 26th 2011.

Evan and Bobby worked hard on Snapchat. But Evan was also a student, and Bobby had a job in a computer company. They did not have a lot of time for the app.

In November 2011, there were 1,000 users on Snapchat, but Bobby and Evan wanted more users.

Evan wanted to advertise Snapchat. He talked to everybody about it: in shops, at the university—everywhere he went. And he gave everyone lessons on the app. He showed them new things on it. Now users could write messages on their photos. And they could draw on their photos, too.

Slowly, lots of people started talking about "Evan's app," and there were new Snapchat users. Soon there were 20,000 users!

A lot of high-school students started using Snapchat. They loved sending funny photos to their friends. Snapchat was different from other social media apps. It was a new app, and students' parents did not use it. Some social-media sites keep their users' photos. But people change, and sometimes they do not want to see their old photos.

Snapchat did not keep any photos. The photos were there for seconds, and then they disappeared. And it showed funny, not beautiful, pictures of people. Everybody liked that.

And Snapchat groups are usually small. You can only add your friends, and you have to know their phone numbers.

Snapchat's interface, 2012

People really liked Snapchat, and Evan and Bobby were very happy about this. In April 2012, there were 100,000 users on Snapchat every day. But the app now needed a lot of work, and they did not have much money.

Evan tried to find some more money for Snapchat, and he asked an old university teacher for help. Then a company with money found Evan. The company was called Lightspeed. It gave Snapchat some money, and now Evan and Bobby could work on the app again.

Now Snapchat had the money it needed. Evan could stop studying and start working at Snapchat every day.

He did the same thing as Steve Jobs from Apple, Bill Gates from Microsoft, and Mark Zuckerberg from Facebook. He left university before he

Steve Jobs **Bill Gates**

Mark Zuckerberg

finished studying. It was only weeks before the end of the university year. Bobby stopped working for the computer company, too, and he started working at Snapchat every day with Evan.

Things looked good for Snapchat. But other companies wanted to help Snapchat with money, and Lightspeed stopped Snapchat from taking their money. Evan was angry about this.

A lawyer helped Evan and Bobby **fight** Lightspeed, but they had to give part of Snapchat to Lightspeed. This was bad for Snapchat. Evan and Bobby learned a very important lesson: to not put their names on documents before understanding them. And Evan always told people that.

CHAPTER FOUR
A lot of money from Facebook

One day, Reggie wrote to Evan. He had some lawyers working for him. He was happy for Evan, but he wanted some of Snapchat's money. Evan and Bobby pushed him out the company, and now Reggie wanted to tell everybody about it.

Evan and Bobby were not happy about this. They asked for help from an important lawyer.

Reggie was not at Evan's twenty-second birthday party in June that year. It was the start of a very long **fight** between Reggie, and Evan and Bobby.

Snapchat got money from other people at that time. Evan's father, John Spiegel, and Michael Lynton, from the company Sony Entertainment, gave Evan and Bobby money. Michael Lynton's daughters went to Evan's old school, and they loved using Snapchat. Lynton had lots of good ideas for Snapchat. He told Evan about them, and this helped Evan with the company.

With more money and more users, Evan and Bobby needed more people to work for Snapchat. Evan had some good student friends. They could write code. He also found other very good people for important jobs at Snapchat. But they **still** worked on the

Michael Lynton

app from Evan's family house. And they still sat at the dining room table with their computers. Things had to change!

At first, iPhones were the only smartphones. But then Nokia and other companies started making smartphones, too. Now lots of people had smartphones. People liked them because they could take photos easily. More people started using the photo apps Instagram and Snapchat on their smartphones. They could take photos of things everywhere and **share** the photos using the apps.

In summer 2012, more than 10,000 new people joined Snapchat every day. There were now

1 million Snapchat users, and they wanted to send photos to their friends quickly with their smartphones. Snapchat was now too big for Evan's family house, and Evan found an office for the company. The first Snapchat office, with its famous logo, was in Venice, in Los Angeles. This was different from other computer companies. They are all in a place called Silicon Valley that is famous for computer and internet companies.

The first Snapchat office

Back in April 2012, Facebook's Mark Zuckerberg bought Instagram for $1 **billion**. Then he wanted to buy Snapchat, too. On November 28th 2012, Zuckerberg sent an email to Evan. Then Zuckerberg came to Los Angeles and met Evan and Bobby. He wanted to buy Snapchat for $60 million, and he wanted Evan and Bobby to stay with the company. Evan and Bobby said no.

Then Zuckerberg showed Evan and Bobby Poke. It was a new Facebook app for messages, disappearing photos and videos.

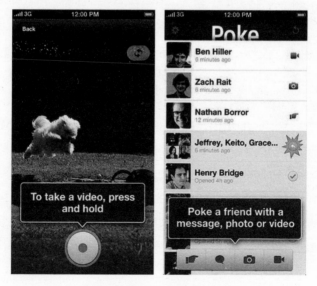

Facebook's Poke app

The app was ready. Evan and Bobby could choose: join Facebook or have a fight with Facebook. They chose a fight!

On December 14th 2012, Snapchat added video to their app. Now users could open the app, make a video with their smartphone camera, and send it to their friends. It was quicker and easier to use than other video apps.

On December 21st 2012, Zuckerberg sent the new Poke app to Evan with the message: "I hope you enjoy Poke."

Poke was the same as Snapchat. But what could Snapchat do about it? Zuckerberg and Facebook were bigger, stronger, and richer than Snapchat. Evan sent a short message to the newspapers: "Welcome, Facebook. Seriously."

The message was nice, but the big fight between Evan Spiegel and Mark Zuckerberg began that Christmas. People were with their friends and family. They used social media a lot. They took lots of photos, and they made videos.

For a week, more people used Poke than used Snapchat.

But Facebook's users are older than Snapchat users, and they do not make a lot of videos. The Facebook users quickly stopped using Poke, but Snapchat's younger users did not stop using Snapchat. They loved it!

Zuckerberg did not buy Snapchat, and Snapchat's users did not move to Facebook. More app users started using Snapchat, not Facebook.

CHAPTER FIVE

Good and bad days

Not everything went well for Snapchat at that time. Reggie came back. In February 2013, his lawyers sent an important document to Evan and Bobby's lawyers. Reggie wanted money from the company, and his lawyers planned to get it for him.

Reggie, Evan and Bobby, and their lawyers met in April. Reggie did not answer the lawyers' questions well, and he did not look good. But Evan and Bobby looked bad because they chose money and not their friend. The fight with Reggie went on.

But not everything went badly. In May 2013, there were 10 million Snapchat users. More companies gave money to Snapchat, and Evan and Bobby got $20 million. Evan bought a red Ferrari car and started learning how to fly a plane. Bobby bought a big new house in Venice, Los Angeles. It cost $2 million.

They were rich now, but they still worked hard every day. They moved to a bigger office that was in a quieter part of Venice. More new people came to work at the company. Some of those people came from big, important companies. Others were young people in their first jobs.

Snapchat users always wanted more from the app. Now they wanted to send group messages— messages to lots of people—but Evan was not happy about this. People could send group messages on other social-media sites. Evan liked the small, friendly side of Snapchat. He did not want it to be the same as other messaging apps.

Then, in October 2013, Snapchat Stories was born. Snapchat users were able to share photos and videos with lots of people, but Snapchat only kept them for twenty-four hours. Users could tell a story through **posting** lots of photos and videos.

Mark Zuckerberg wanted to buy Snapchat again. This time he wanted to pay Evan and Bobby $3 billion for it! How could Evan and Bobby say no to $3 billion? It was a lot of money.

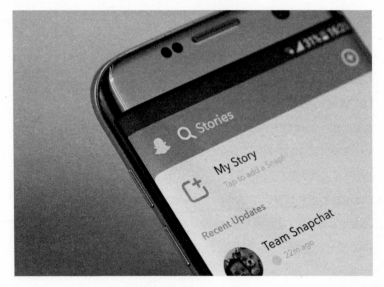

Snapchat Stories

But could Evan and Bobby work for Facebook? No, they could not! They said "no" to Mark Zuckerberg again. They wanted Snapchat to stay the same. They did not want it to be a small part of the Facebook company.

Evan and Bobby were not $3 billion richer, but things still looked very good for Snapchat.

Then bad days came at about the same time as Evan and Bobby said no to Facebook. A group of researchers got Snapchat users' names and phone numbers. They told Snapchat and their users about this problem on Christmas Day 2013, but Snapchat did nothing about it.

On January 1st 2014, a group of **hackers** called Gibson Security posted the phone numbers and usernames of over 4.6 million Snapchat users on the internet. The newspapers were not kind about Evan and his company, because he did not say sorry to the Snapchat users.

CHAPTER SIX

How can we make money?

On February 19th 2014, Facebook bought the WhatsApp messaging app for $19 billion. Facebook now had Instagram and WhatsApp, and it was stronger than before. Snapchat's fight with Facebook was still happening!

People loved using Snapchat, but the question Evan asked was, "How can we make money?" In 2014, more than 100 people worked for Snapchat. There were lots of different groups in the company. The money-making group had the most people, and it grew the fastest. Evan wanted Snapchat to make money!

From May 1st 2014, Snapchat users could also video call and send text messages to their friends, not only send them videos and photos. Users liked this, but it still did not make any money for Snapchat. This was because not many companies advertised on Snapchat.

In September 2014, Snapchat bought Scan. Scan was a QR code company. You find QR codes on things in supermarkets. A computer reads the code, and then you pay for the thing. People could use Scan and make their own QR code. These were called Snapcodes. Now Snapchat users could use other people's Snapcodes to add them as friends. Snapchat wants its users to find things and buy them on the internet with Snapcodes. But for now they cannot do this, and Snapcodes do not make any money for Snapchat.

Scanning a QR code with a smartphone

Evan and Bobby wanted to work on their app and make more money, but they really needed to stop the fight with Reggie. It took a lot of their time and cost a lot of money. In the end, the lawyers found an answer. Evan and Bobby paid Reggie $157.5 million, and Snapchat wrote in the newspapers: "Disappearing photos were Reggie Brown's idea, and he worked on the app at the start."

Reggie took the money, but he could never speak to the newspapers about Snapchat again. The fight with Reggie was finished. But the fight with Facebook was not.

In June 2014, Facebook started a new photo app called Slingshot. Slingshot users could send a photo to a friend. Then the friend had to send a photo back. Nobody liked the new app.

Slingshot, Facebook's new photo app

At the same time, Snapchat started Snapchat Live at the Electric Daisy Carnival. Lots of music bands were there. Snapchat posted photos and videos of the **event**, and Snapchat users did, too. Snapchat users everywhere could watch the bands play live (at the same time as the bands played) through the eyes of other Snapchat users.

People making videos on their smartphones at a music event

It was also possible to add geofilters to photos and videos. Geofilters tell you the name of the place or the event. Snapchat quickly designed geofilters for cities, universities, and coffee shops. And people could design their own geofilters and send them to Snapchat. People loved using Snapchat Live and geofilters!

Snapchat's geofilters

There was a beautiful story at the University of Wisconsin. A girl saw a boy on the university's Live Story and wanted to find him. She liked him but did not know his name. He liked football and wore a Vikings American football shirt.

The girl posted a Live Story on Snapchat. Friends started posting videos and pictures of the boy and the girl to the story, too. Then the pair met at a university bar. Snapchat made a special love story geofilter for the boy and girl.

still a better love story than twilight

THEY MET

HELP VIKINGS FAN FIND MYSTERY GIRL

VIKING FAN ARRIVED!

The love story geofilter

On December 31st 2014, Snapchat made a Live Story about parties for the New Year across the world. People started making wonderful Live Stories about lots of different events: sports, music, film and TV, or other daily things. But this still did not make any money for Snapchat.

Snapchat had to make its money from advertising. But how could it get more companies to advertise on the app? Snapchat had a lot of young users. Companies could not easily advertise to young people, because young people did not watch a lot of TV. So companies started to advertise on Snapchat. First, a film company posted a twenty-second video. It was a Snapchat story and advertised a film called *Ouija*. Millions of users watched the video.

Then the company Samsung made a Live Story at a famous music event. Snapchat showed the bands getting ready before they played. This was new because these parts of an event are not usually on TV.

More and more companies started advertising through Live Stories at important events, and between 10 and 20 million people watched them. Now Snapchat began making money!

CHAPTER SEVEN

People on Snapchat

Evan always loved music, and he wanted to start a Snapchat music company. Snapchat could not make music, but it could show new music videos. In February 2015, the **singer** Madonna posted the first music video on Snapchat. It was the same as other users' **posts**. People could only watch it for twenty-four hours, but it was something new for Snapchat users.

After that, users could see four new videos by the singer Goldroom on Snapchat. Users could watch the videos easily because he filmed them to look good on a smartphone. His videos looked the same as people's videos from music events.

Evan also liked writing. Now he wanted to give people news on Snapchat. In January 2015, Snapchat started Discover. It gave users news stories from different companies: CNN, *Cosmopolitan*, *National Geographic*, and Yahoo News.

Other companies did not want to put their news on Discover. They could not take users from Snapchat to their company websites, and they had to make special videos for smartphones. Users did not really like Discover. Snapchat designed Discover again in July 2015, and again in June 2016. It was better, but it was still not as good as Live Stories.

Snapchat is different from other social-media sites because you do not "like" what people post. And it is more about your friends than about famous people. But there are lots of famous Snapchat users, and they can make the app look special.

DJ Khaled is famous in the music world. A friend told him about Snapchat in 2015. He started filming every minute of his day and posting it on Snapchat. He also talked on Snapchat about the good things you can do every day. These things could help you feel happy. He is different from other famous people. He says lots of funny things. Snapchat users like him, and 6 million people started watching DJ Khaled's stories on Snapchat.

DJ Khaled

People get famous, too, because other users like the photos they share. Snapchat user Shonduras traveled a lot for his job. He sent his six sisters photos of places everywhere he went. And he added drawings to his photos. His sisters liked his photos, and lots of other people liked them, too.

Shonduras

A teacher from Boston heard about Snapchat from his students. He also started sending photos on Snapchat with the name MPlatco, and he drew pictures of famous people from TV. He drew Doctor Who and Harry Potter. People loved his photos and drawings, too. Shonduras and MPlatco left their jobs because they were so good on Snapchat.

Now they work for lots of different film and TV companies. They use Snapchat every day for their jobs.

One of the most famous Snapchat users is a doctor. His name is Dr. Miami. He helps people with their bodies and their faces. He posts pictures of them on Snapchat. People love his posts! In 2016, 1 million people watched Dr. Miami's stories every day, and lots of people wanted his help.

Mackenzie Stith also wants to help people through Snapchat. She posts things about her days. Sometimes Mackenzie feels sad, and sometimes she feels frightened. She tells other young Snapchat users about it. This helps her, and it helps other people, too. People get famous on Snapchat because of their posts. But posting their stories helps them, too.

CHAPTER EIGHT

Snapchat's secrets

In November 2014, hackers got into Sony Entertainment's company computers. This was bad for Sony. It was also bad for Evan Spiegel, because he sent lots of emails to Michael Lynton at Sony. Snapchat was in the newspapers again, and Evan was not happy about this. He wrote a message on the social-media site Twitter about "keeping secrets."

I've been feeling a lot of things since our business plans were made public last night. Definitely angry. Definitely devastated. I felt like I was going to cry all morning, so I went on a walk and thought through a couple of things.

Evan's post on Twitter

Every good company needs secrets. Secrets help companies grow and make new things before other companies learn about them. But Snapchat has more secrets than other companies. People at

Snapchat cannot talk about their work to their friends and family. Evan does not like meeting people in offices. He likes walking and talking on the beach. Nobody can hear you there. And he does not tell many people about his new ideas for Snapchat. They are his secrets.

There are special groups at Snapchat with ten people in them. Every Wednesday night, these groups meet at the Snapchat offices.

Sometimes they talk about work. Are things going well or going badly? Sometimes they do things together: they play sport, sing, paint, or go out.

Sometimes they do things for other people. They cook and give food to poor people, or help them in their homes.

In these groups, you have to say true things. You have to listen to other people. But you cannot talk to other people about it later. People have to keep other people's secrets. Evan got this idea from his old high school, and it is an important part of the Snapchat company today.

Snapchat users enjoy using the app. And most people enjoy working for Snapchat, too. The company has lots of good parties for them. And they can take their friends and families to these parties.

Snapchat's first birthday party

But some people start to work at Snapchat and then leave quickly. Maybe this is because things change very quickly at the company. We do not know. These are also Snapchat's secrets.

CHAPTER NINE

Companies advertise on Snapchat

Snapchat is always thinking of new ideas because it wants to make the app better.

In September 2015, Snapchat added new camera lenses to the app. You take photos through a camera lens. Users could choose different lenses for their photographs.

Snapchat lenses

One lens could help you look more beautiful. One lens could make you look uglier. Other lenses could make you look funnier. Users could try new lenses every day, and Snapchat kept users' favorite lenses. For a short time, users could also buy lenses through the app. But Snapchat stopped this because it could make more money through advertising. Companies were able to advertise things on Snapchat for one or two days with special geofilters and lenses.

Film companies used Snapchat's lenses and geofilters because they wanted more people to go to the cinema. Fox Studios advertised their film *The Peanuts Movie*. Users could **become** Snoopy or Woodstock with the special lenses. And they could share them on Snapchat. Fox also advertised the new X-Men film, *X-Men: Apocalypse*. Users could become X-Men with special lenses.

Food and drinks companies also advertised with Snapchat lenses and geofilters. For two days, users could make a video of a Gatorade drink going over their heads at a football event. And users could change their heads into taco shells with Taco Bell's lens.

Evan also wanted Snapchat to make news again. He got a new group of people together and they started making Live Stories about different news events at the end of 2015. They put videos on Snapchat Live and asked people questions. These videos were longer and better than Snapchat's users' videos. But users could still post their own video about news events. And they could add new geofilters to them.

Snapchat also did Live Stories from the Rio Olympic Games in Brazil in 2016. They talked to famous sports people and made videos of them. Users could watch the sports people doing normal things at the Olympic Village. They could also watch them getting ready for the Olympic Games.

Sports people from over the world posted on Snapchat from the Olympics. It was a very big world news story, and lots of people watched it. This was also good news for companies because they could advertise on the Olympics Live Stories. And this was good news for Snapchat because it could make lots of money.

Snapchat today

Today, you can do the same things on Facebook and Instagram as you can on Snapchat. You can post photos, and send people messages and money. And you can watch videos and view stories. But Snapchat's users are not the same as Facebook and Instagram's users. They want different things. Facebook and Instagram users want to keep pictures and videos on the internet. Snapchat users do not.

Mark Zuckerberg wanted Snapchat's users to choose Facebook, but many famous people and companies chose Snapchat. They put pictures with Snapcodes on Twitter and Facebook. Other Snapchat users could use these to add the companies to their Snapchat group. Twitter and Facebook were very angry about this.

But this still did not stop Snapchat from getting bigger. In June 2016, Twitter had 140 million daily users, but Snapchat had 150 million daily users! In August 2016, Instagram started Instagram

Stories. You could only see the stories for twenty-four hours. It was the same as Snapchat Stories, but more people used it.

Facebook started making lenses. They were the same as Snapchat's lenses. And now there are disappearing messages on Instagram and on Facebook Messenger, too.

But Snapchat users are happy. They do not want to move to other social media apps.

Evan is still adding new things to the Snapchat app. Users can send and listen to video messages with Snapchat. They can also speak to people on the phone or by video with the app. This is the same as WhatsApp and Facebook Messenger.

And in July 2016, Snapchat started Memories. With Memories, users can keep photos, videos, and stories on the app for the first time. This is a new idea for Snapchat, but it is not a new idea for Facebook.

In March 2016, Snapchat bought the company

Bitstrips. Users can make their own funny emojis and use them on Snapchat. They are called Bitmoji, and users loved them! Evan wanted his girlfriend to marry him, and she put Bitmojis of her and Evan on Snapchat. The Evan Bitmoji said, "Marry me!"

Evan and his wife, Miranda Kerr

Back in 2014, Snapchat bought the company Vergence Labs for $15 million. Vergence made special glasses you could use to make a video. Evan started Snap Lab in 2014, but at first it was a secret. Snap Lab made some glasses with a camera on them called **Spectacles**. You can wear the glasses and make videos with them.

Evan went on holiday with his girlfriend and took the glasses with him. He walked through the trees and looked up at the sky. He made a video of his holiday.

Back in Los Angeles, Evan watched the video on his computer. He could see and remember everything about his holiday. In September 2016, users could buy Spectacles. Users could make ten-second videos through their own eyes. Then they could post the videos on Snapchat.

At first, Snapchat was only an app for sending disappearing photos to friends. You could take and send photos and videos. Then everybody wanted the Snapchat app because you could do lots of things with it.

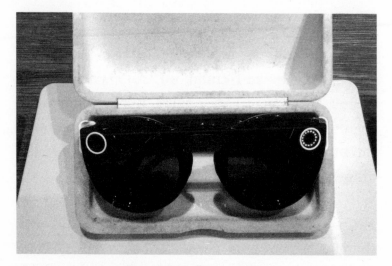

Snapchat Spectacles

**Snapchat's pop-up shop with Spectacles,
in New York**

Today, Snapchat users can advertise, post stories, and use geofilters and lenses. They can keep photos and videos, make Bitmoji, buy things online, and make videos with Spectacles. More than 1,500 people work for Snapchat. And Evan Spiegel is as famous as Mark Zuckerberg and Steve Jobs. But what's next for Snapchat?

Evan wants users to be able to find things, understand things, and make things with Snapchat. He wants users to learn about things and buy those things with the app.

But Snapchat is different from other social-media sites because it does not keep things, and it does not know a lot about its users. So how can it understand them? Does Snapchat have to be the same as Facebook and Instagram and learn more about its users? And can this be a bad thing? Or will social-media sites have to change and be the same as Snapchat one day?

During-reading questions

Write the answers to these questions in your notebook.

CHAPTER ONE

1 When and where was Evan Spiegel born?
2 How was Bobby Murphy different from Evan and Reggie?
3 What did Evan think about Reggie's idea?

CHAPTER TWO

1 How was Picaboo different from other social-media sites?
2 What was Picaboo's logo?
3 Why were Evan and Bobby not happy with Reggie?

CHAPTER THREE

1 Why did Evan and Bobby change the name of the app?
2 Why did a lot of high-school students like Snapchat?
3 Evan did the same thing as Steve Jobs, Bill Gates, and Mark Zuckerberg. What was it?

CHAPTER FOUR

1 What did Reggie Brown want from Evan and Bobby?
2 Who gave Snapchat some money?
3 What did Facebook start on December 21st 2012, and what was the problem with it?

CHAPTER FIVE

1 What new things did Evan and Bobby buy with their $20 million?
2 What could Snapchat users do with Snapchat Stories?
3 What did a group of hackers do to Snapchat in January 2014?

CHAPTER SIX

1 What could Snapchat users do with Snapcodes?
2 What happened to stop the fight with Reggie Brown?
3 What are geofilters, and what could Snapchat users do with them?

CHAPTER SEVEN

1 Which singer posted the first music video on Snapchat?
2 Who is DJ Khaled, and what did he do on Snapchat?
3 How did Shonduras and MPlatco get new jobs through Snapchat?

CHAPTER EIGHT

1 What did Evan Spiegel tweet about in November 2014?
2 What happens every Wednesday night at Snapchat?
3 Why do some people start to work at Snapchat and then leave quickly?

CHAPTER NINE

1 What can you do with Snapchat lenses?
2 Which companies made special Snapchat lenses and geofilters?
3 From which big sports event did Snapchat make Live Stories in 2016?

1 What are Spectacles?
2 What can you do on Snapchat today? List the things that are true in your notebook.

- advertise
- buy things online
- draw emojis
- keep photos and videos
- "like" posts
- share photos
- view stories

- send messages
- send money
- send video messages
- speak by video
- speak on the phone
- watch videos

After-reading questions

1 What new things did you learn about Snapchat?
2 What do you think about the people in the book now?
3 Do you think Evan, Bobby, and Reggie could be friends again one day? Why/Why not?
4 Could you say no to $3 billion? Why/Why not?
5 Why do young people like Snapchat more than they like other social-media sites?
6 Snapchat does not know a lot about its users now. Is this a good thing or a bad thing?
7 Do other social-media sites know too much about us? Do they have to change?

Exercises

1 Complete these sentences in your notebook, using the words from the box.

> lawyers   computer   designed   parties   joined
>   company   newspaper   university

1 Evan's parents were ....*lawyers*.....
2 Evan built his first .... at the age of eleven.
3 Evan wrote for the school ....
4 Evan asked the drinks .... Red Bull for a job.
5 Evan .... things for computers at Stanford University.
6 Evan and Reggie met at ....
7 Reggie liked ...., too.
8 Evan, Reggie, and Bobby .... the Kappa Sigma club.

2 Write *E* for Evan, *R* for Reggie, or *B* for Bobby in your notebook.

1 He lived with his father in a very big and expensive house, and he had lots of parties there. ...*E*...
2 He studied English at Stanford University.
3 He studied mathematics and computers at Stanford University.
4 He was born on January 17th 1990, in South Carolina, in the south of the United States.
5 He was born on June 4th 1990, in Los Angeles, California.
6 His mother comes from the Philippines, but he was born in California on July 19th 1988.

3 **Write the correct verbs in your notebook.**

1 Bobby **make** / *made* a website with Evan.

2 Evan **ask** / **asked** students from the Kappa Sigma club for help with their website.

3 There **is** / **was** nothing really new about the website.

4 Things did not **go** / **went** well for Evan and Reggie.

5 One day Reggie **had** / **have** an idea for a social-media site.

6 He **think** / **thought**, "I'd like to send disappearing photos!"

7 Evan listened and said, "That **is** / **was** a million-dollar idea!"

8 Because the website was not very good, they **build** / **built** a phone app.

CHAPTER TWO

4 **In your notebook, match the words to the definitions.**

Example: 1–c

1 app   **a** It is a special computer language.

2 code   **b** Social-media sites have lots of these.

3 document   **c** You have these on your smartphone. They do different jobs for you.

4 iPhones   **d** A company's special picture.

5 logo   **e** Apple make these.

6 passwords   **f** An important bit of paper.

7 users   **g** You can open things with these secret numbers or letters.

5 **Who does these things on Snapchat? Write the correct names in your notebook.**

| Goldroom | DJ Khaled | Dr. Miami |
| Mackenzie Stith | MPlatco | Shonduras |

1 ....*Goldroom*...... posts music videos on Snapchat.

2 .... says lots of funny things on Snapchat.

3 .... adds drawings to his photos.

4 .... draws pictures of famous people from TV.

5 .... posts pictures of people's bodies and faces on Snapchat.

6 .... tells other young Snapchat users about feeling sad or frightened.

CHAPTER NINE

6 **Complete these sentences in your notebook, using the comparative form of the adjective.**

Snapchat is always thinking of new ideas because it wants to make the app [1] .....*better*... (good). In September 2015, Snapchat added new camera lenses to the app. One lens could help you look [2] .... (beautiful). One lens could make you look [3] .... (ugly). Other lenses could make you look [4] .... (funny). Users could try new lenses every day, and Snapchat kept people's favorite lenses. For a short time, users could also buy lenses through the app. But Snapchat stopped this because it could become [5] .... (rich) through advertising. Companies were able to advertise things on Snapchat for [6] .... (long), with special geofilters and lenses.

CHAPTER TEN

7 **Put these words in the correct group in your notebook.**

> Facebook   geofilters   Instagram   lenses
>   Snapchat Stories   Twitter   Snapchat

Social media apps	Parts of apps
Facebook	*lenses*

Project work

1 Write a newspaper report about one of the people on page 19 of this book. Look for the answers to these questions online:
- When and where was he born?
- What did he study?
- How did he get his big idea?
- What happened next?
- What is he doing now?

2 Write a different ending to the book. Evan and Bobby say yes to $3 billion from Facebook. What happens to them and to Snapchat?

3 Write a review of an app you really like. In your review say:
- what you can do with the app
- why you like using it
- why it is better than other apps
- what other things you would like to do with the app.

An answer key for all questions and exercises can be found at **www.penguinreaders.co.uk**

Glossary

advertise (v.)
to tell people about something
because you want them to buy
or use it

app (n.)
You have an *app* on your phone.
It helps you do things on your
phone.

be born (v.)
(Past simple: **was born**)
When a baby *is born*, it comes
out of its mother's body. When
a thing *is born*, people can use it
for the first time.

become (v.)
to start to be something

billion (n.)
the number 1,000,000,000

club (n.)
A *club* is a group of people.
They do something together
and often meet at the same
time every week.

code (n.); **coder** (n.)
An *app* or *website* works from
code. *Code* is a language of letters,
numbers and symbols (= <> * }).

company (n.)
A *company* makes and sells things.
People work for a *company*.

design (v.)
to plan how a thing will look
and work

disappearing (adj.)
You can only see *disappearing*
things for a short time. After
that, you cannot see them.

document (n.)
an important paper

event (n.)
A football game or party is an
event. People go to events and
enjoy them.

fight (v. and n.)
You *fight* very hard because
you want something from a
person or company, or you
want to stop them from doing
something. You have a *fight*
with them.

funny (adj.)
People laugh at a *funny* person
or thing.

hacker (n.)
Hackers take people's names,
addresses and phone numbers
from a computer. They can do
bad things with them.

high school (n.)
People go to *high school* between thirteen and eighteen years old.

idea (n.)
when you think of a thing

iPhone (n.)
A name for a phone. A company called Apple makes it.

join (v.)
to do something with other people

lawyer (n.)
A *lawyer* helps people with the law (= the things they can and cannot do in their country).

logo (n.)
A small picture. A *logo advertises* a *company*.

million (n.)
the number 1,000,000

newspaper (n.)
You read about the news in a *newspaper*.

password (n.)
A group of letters and numbers. You put these letters and numbers into your phone or computer. Then you can use it.

post (v. and n.)
You *post* a photo or message on the internet. Your photo or message is called a *post*.

share (v.)
to put photos, videos, or messages on the internet for other people to see

singer (n.)
A *singer* sings songs for money.

social-media site (n.)
Facebook and Twitter are *social-media sites*. You *post* messages, photos and videos on them, and your friends can see your *posts*.

spectacles (n.)
Spectacles are glasses. In this story, '*Spectacles*' is the name of some special glasses with a camera on them. You can wear the glasses and make videos with them.

still (adv.)
Something that is *still* happening is happening until now.

university (n.)
People leave *high school* and go to *university*.

user (n.)
A *user* uses an *app* or *website*.

version (n.)
A *version* of something is that
thing with some different parts.
The *version* of the Snapchat *logo*
in this book is a bit different to
the first Snapchat *logo*.

website (n.)
You look at a *website* on the
internet. It tells you about
something.

Penguin 🐧 Readers

Visit **www.penguinreaders.co.uk**
for FREE Penguin Readers resources
and digital and audio versions of this book.